This Book Belongs To:

_____

Breathing Space: a coloring book of mindful moments

ISBN 978-1-7362347-0-9

Published by House of Gentileschi - www.houseofgentileschi.com

For my Beloved Markus, who fills my
life with love and kindness every
day of my life.

Hello!

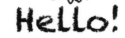

Welcome to your very own Breathing Space.
Oh yes, this is much more than just a coloring book!
This is a quiet break all your own, to sit and ponder all
the things that make you the incredibly wonderful
person you are. Each page of this book is illustrated with
an image created to reflect a personal aspect that you
have in abundance. While coloring, you are invited to take
some time to meditate upon these characteristics and
consider how you manifest each one in your daily life. Let
your mind wander free, and revel in the warmth of all
your admirable qualities.

You are encouraged to color in any way that makes you
happy and to color with all the creativity you have inside
that marvelous mind of yours. For example, if flowers can
be any color, then so can people! Pink, lavender, teal, or
even spring green, all make for delightful skin tones in
this realm of relaxation and contemplation. But feel free to
explore any other color that tickles your fancy at any
given moment! To very loosely paraphrase the luminary Dr.
Martin Luther King, Jr., the focus here is not on the color of
one's skin, but the content of one's character.

As you make your way through this little book, let it serve
as a guide to reacquaint yourself with, and deepen your
connection to, your profoundly amazing character. So
gather your pencils and a cup of your favorite tea, find a
nice, peaceful place to color, and enjoy the Breathing Space
you so rightly deserve.

With love,

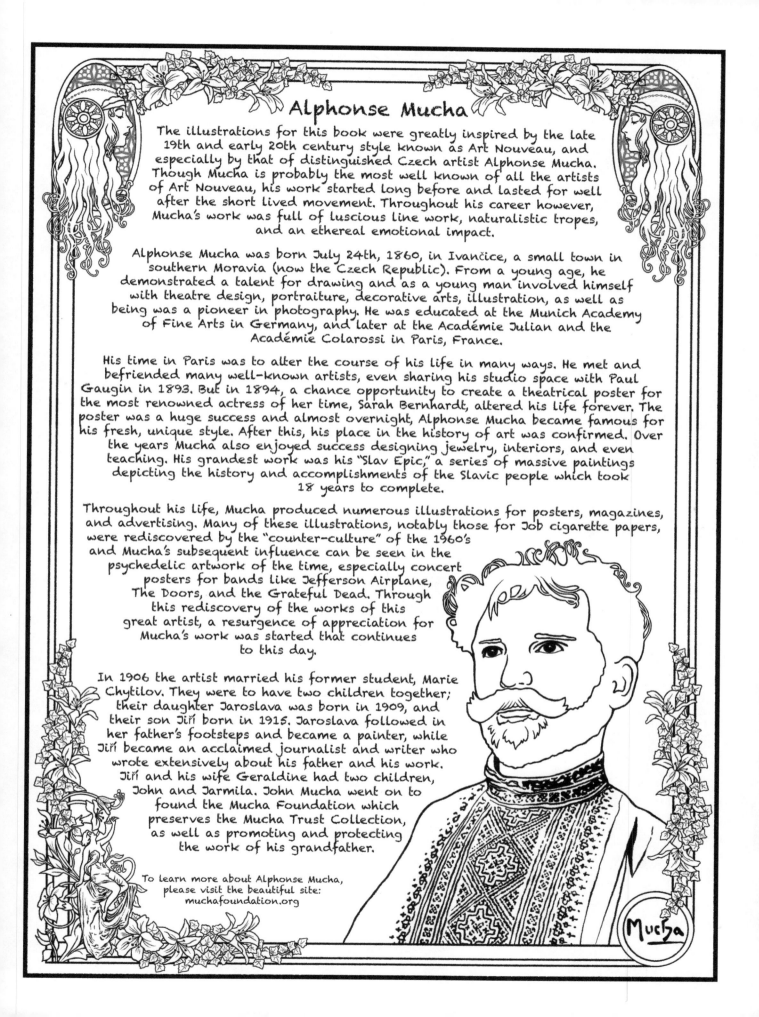

Alphonse Mucha

The illustrations for this book were greatly inspired by the late 19th and early 20th century style known as Art Nouveau, and especially by that of distinguished Czech artist Alphonse Mucha. Though Mucha is probably the most well known of all the artists of Art Nouveau, his work started long before and lasted for well after the short lived movement. Throughout his career however, Mucha's work was full of luscious line work, naturalistic tropes, and an ethereal emotional impact.

Alphonse Mucha was born July 24th, 1860, in Ivančice, a small town in southern Moravia (now the Czech Republic). From a young age, he demonstrated a talent for drawing and as a young man involved himself with theatre design, portraiture, decorative arts, illustration, as well as being was a pioneer in photography. He was educated at the Munich Academy of Fine Arts in Germany, and later at the Académie Julian and the Académie Colarossi in Paris, France.

His time in Paris was to alter the course of his life in many ways. He met and befriended many well-known artists, even sharing his studio space with Paul Gaugin in 1893. But in 1894, a chance opportunity to create a theatrical poster for the most renowned actress of her time, Sarah Bernhardt, altered his life forever. The poster was a huge success and almost overnight, Alphonse Mucha became famous for his fresh, unique style. After this, his place in the history of art was confirmed. Over the years Mucha also enjoyed success designing jewelry, interiors, and even teaching. His grandest work was his "Slav Epic," a series of massive paintings depicting the history and accomplishments of the Slavic people which took 18 years to complete.

Throughout his life, Mucha produced numerous illustrations for posters, magazines, and advertising. Many of these illustrations, notably those for Job cigarette papers, were rediscovered by the "counter-culture" of the 1960's and Mucha's subsequent influence can be seen in the psychedelic artwork of the time, especially concert posters for bands like Jefferson Airplane, The Doors, and the Grateful Dead. Through this rediscovery of the works of this great artist, a resurgence of appreciation for Mucha's work was started that continues to this day.

In 1906 the artist married his former student, Marie Chytilov. They were to have two children together; their daughter Jaroslava was born in 1909, and their son Jiří born in 1915. Jaroslava followed in her father's footsteps and became a painter, while Jiří became an acclaimed journalist and writer who wrote extensively about his father and his work. Jiří and his wife Geraldine had two children, John and Jarmila. John Mucha went on to found the Mucha Foundation which preserves the Mucha Trust Collection, as well as promoting and protecting the work of his grandfather.

To learn more about Alphonse Mucha, please visit the beautiful site: muchafoundation.org

As you color your way through the following pages, you are warmly invited to start each one by taking a moment to consider each theme presented. Then, while you are happily coloring away, you could try thinking to yourself something like, "Wow. I am so abundant in...(whatever the theme might be)," or "Wow. I am so grateful for all my...(whatever the theme might be)." Those are just two examples of course. Feel free to use them or make up your very own coloring mantras. Awesome as you are, there is no doubt they will be effective and eloquent!

1

Creativity

2

Playfulness

3

Authenticity

4

Connectedness

5

Reliability

6

Empathy

7

Compassion

Encouragement

9

Courageousness

Gentleness

11

Fairness

12

Generosity

Forgiveness

14

Kindness

15

Honesty

Integrity

17

Humility

18

Lovingness

19

Loyalty

20

Openness

21

Optimism

Perseverance

Respectfulness

Responsibility

Self-Discipline

Thoughtfulness

27

Vulnerability

Trust

29

Patience

30

Self-Care

The majority of the illustrations in this book are a varying mixture of imaginary people. However there are two illustrations that are of special note as they are of real people who led truly inspirational lives.

The first is the illustration created for "Perseverance." This image is of the the Arapaho woman known as Pretty Nose, born around 1851 and who some say lived to be over 109 years old. In 1876, after the US Government broke their treaty by violently taking lands promised to the Arapaho, Lakota, and Dakota people, Pretty Nose participated in defending her people at the Battle of Little Bighorn. One can only imagine how much inner strength she called upon as she witnessed so much dramatic change over her long life. Through it all however, she remained true to herself and to the traditions of her people. Her legacy is that same strength and dedication passed down through the generations of her family, such as her great grandson Mark Soldier Wolf (who was a US veteran and the first historian for the Arapaho tribe), as well as her great-great granddaughter Yufna Soldier Wolf (who is an activist and served as the director of Northern Arapaho Tribal Historic Preservation). It is through her descendants that the perseverance of the illustrious warrior, matriarch, and historical icon named Pretty Nose lives on to this day.

The second illustration, created to represent "Gentleness," is based on a 1926 photograph of the lovely and courageous Danish painter, model, and LGBTQ pioneer Lili Elbe. Lili was born male in 1882 in Vejle, Denmark but began living as a woman around 1912 in Paris. She suffered from what today we understand to be gender dysphoria, and even possibly Klinefelter Syndrome (where a male is born with two X chromosomes and one Y chromosome, instead of the common XY chromosomes). Not finding merely dressing as a woman fulfilling, Lili decided to become the first person to undergo what was then highly experimental transition surgery in 1930. Lili's story had nearly been forgotten until the mid-twentieth century when her memoir, written under the pseudonym "Niels Hoyer" and entitled "Man Into Woman," was rediscovered and republished, directly inspiring other transgender people such as historian Jan Morris and tennis player Renee Richards on their own journeys. In 2000, David Ebershoff wrote a fictionalized biography of Lili's life entitled "The Danish Girl" which was made into a film of the same name in 2015. Lili's courageous dedication to remaining gently steadfast to her quest to become her true self remains as inspiring today as it did in her own time.

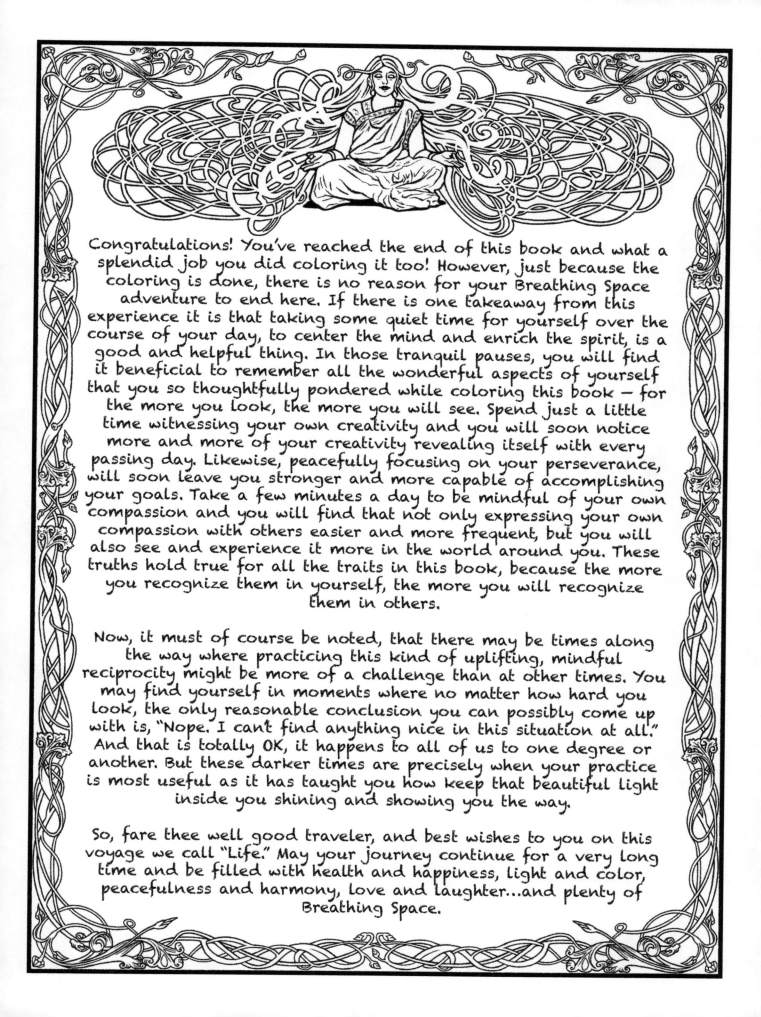

Congratulations! You've reached the end of this book and what a splendid job you did coloring it too! However, just because the coloring is done, there is no reason for your Breathing Space adventure to end here. If there is one takeaway from this experience it is that taking some quiet time for yourself over the course of your day, to center the mind and enrich the spirit, is a good and helpful thing. In those tranquil pauses, you will find it beneficial to remember all the wonderful aspects of yourself that you so thoughtfully pondered while coloring this book — for the more you look, the more you will see. Spend just a little time witnessing your own creativity and you will soon notice more and more of your creativity revealing itself with every passing day. Likewise, peacefully focusing on your perseverance, will soon leave you stronger and more capable of accomplishing your goals. Take a few minutes a day to be mindful of your own compassion and you will find that not only expressing your own compassion with others easier and more frequent, but you will also see and experience it more in the world around you. These truths hold true for all the traits in this book, because the more you recognize them in yourself, the more you will recognize them in others.

Now, it must of course be noted, that there may be times along the way where practicing this kind of uplifting, mindful reciprocity might be more of a challenge than at other times. You may find yourself in moments where no matter how hard you look, the only reasonable conclusion you can possibly come up with is, "Nope. I can't find anything nice in this situation at all." And that is totally OK, it happens to all of us to one degree or another. But these darker times are precisely when your practice is most useful as it has taught you how keep that beautiful light inside you shining and showing you the way.

So, fare thee well good traveler, and best wishes to you on this voyage we call "Life." May your journey continue for a very long time and be filled with health and happiness, light and color, peacefulness and harmony, love and laughter...and plenty of Breathing Space.